NAPOLE

FREEDOM FROM YOUR

FEARS

GAIN A NEW PERSPECTIVE AND SEE THE OPPORTUNITY AROUND YOU

Published and distributed by:

SOUND WISDOM
P.O. Box 310
Shippensburg, PA 17257-0310

717-530-2122

info@soundwisdom.com

www.soundwisdom.com

While efforts have been made to verify information contained in this publication, neither the author nor the publisher assumes any responsibility for errors, inaccuracies, or omissions. While this publication is chock-full of useful, practical information; it is not intended to be legal or accounting advice. All readers are advised to seek competent lawyers and accountants to follow laws and regulations that may apply to specific situations. The reader of this publication assumes responsibility for the use of the information. The author and publisher assume no responsibility or liability whatsoever on the behalf of the reader of this publication.

ISBN 13 TP: 978-1-64095-230-0

ISBN 13 eBook: 978-1-64095-231-7

For Worldwide Distribution, Printed in the U.S.A.

1 2 3 4 5 6 7 8 / 25 24 23 22 21

FREEDOM FROM YOUR

FEARS

If there was ever a time in this country when men and women need to recognize the power of their own minds, when they need to overcome frustration and fear, that time is now. There is too much fear spread around, too many people talking about depressions. ...Let's get our minds, each and every one of us as individuals, fixed upon a definite goal so big and so outstanding that we'll have no time to think about these things we don't want.

—**Napoleon Hill,** "Maker of Miracle Men," 1952

CONTENTS

CHAPTER 1

FEAR IS A MINDSET

Before you control conditions, you must control yourself.

—**Napoleon Hill,** *Think and Grow Rich*

THERE is no emotion more pernicious than fear. It can make us feel like the ground has been pulled out from underneath us and we are spiraling out of control. It can cause us to question our understanding of ourselves and the world. It roots itself deep in the subconscious and darkens our dominating thoughts, coloring our perceptions and, in turn, our actions. However, fear is simply a feeling—one that can be mastered and channeled to work for, rather than against, us.

Filled with advice from Napoleon Hill, whose landmark book *Think and Grow Rich* helped raise a generation out of the despondency and paralysis brought on by depression and world war and has since made more millionaires and influencers than any other, this book will help you enlarge your perspective so that you can regain control over your life. Perspective means the difference between whether defeat is final or fortuitous—whether you allow fear to hold you back from your dreams or use it as fuel to pursue them doggedly.

> Perspective means the difference between whether defeat is final or fortuitous.

MINDSET MATTERS

When we experience difficulty, it is easy to look around at those who have "made it" and assume that their road to success was not paved with obstacles similar to, or worse than, our own. With only the end result of success visible to us, we resent others' "good luck" and bemoan our own "misfortune." We excuse our indecision and acceptance of defeat as the result of "fate" or circumstances outside our control, when really these are alibis concealing deep-seated fears. Challenging our narrow perspective, Napoleon Hill writes:

"Those who succeed usually are called "lucky." To be sure, they are lucky! But, learn the facts and you will discover that their "luck" consists of that secret power from within, which they have applied through a Positive Mental Attitude; a determination to follow the road of Faith instead of the road of Fear and self-limitation.

The power that comes from within recognizes no such reality as permanent barriers.

It converts defeat into a challenge of greater effort.

It removes self-imposed limitations such as fear and doubt.

And, above all else let us remember that it makes no black marks against any man's record which he cannot erase.

If approached through the power from within, every day brings forth a newly born opportunity for individual achievement which need not in any way whatsoever be burdened by the failures of yesterday.

It favors no race or creed, and it is bound by no sort of arbitrary consistency compelling man to remain in poverty because he was born in poverty.[1]"

As Hill discovered after 25 years of interviewing and studying the lives of over 500 of America's most successful businesspeople and thought leaders, almost every person of great achievement had, in fact, experienced significant setbacks on their path to success. What separated those who "made it" from those who succumbed to defeat or mediocrity was not personal advantages like education, connections, and money, but rather the ability to persevere through challenges and remain steadfast in their pursuit of their definite chief aim. This boils down to one key element: one's *state of mind*. Thus was born a science of success philosophy founded upon one central tenet: *Your thoughts dictate your results.*

James J. Hill, the railroad executive responsible for the transcontinental railroad system; Andrew Carnegie, the great steel magnate; Henry Ford, the automobile pioneer, Lee De Forest, the "father of radio"; and the renowned inventor Thomas A. Edison—we revere these giants of industry, admiring them for their genius and apparent good fortune. But as Hill explains, genius is not an innate quality that some people are born with and others must do without. According to Hill, it is nothing more than the application of the "secret power from within which is available to everyone who will embrace it and use it."[2] He continues:

"

We all know of the achievements of these great leaders...

But, unfortunately, not all of us recognize the handicaps under which they worked, the obstacles they had to overcome, and the spirit of active faith in which they carried on their work.

Of this we may be sure, however: *Their achievements were in exact proportion to the emergencies they had to overcome!* [3]

Faith, self-confidence, creativity—these three attributes, all interrelated, derive from one source: a *positive mental attitude*, the crucial trait that ensures the success of the world's top achievers. As Hill establishes:

when you come right down to the circumstances which lift some men to high stations in life and condemn others to penury and want, the likelihood is that their widely separated positions reflect their respective mental attitudes. The high man chooses the high road of Faith, the low man chooses the low road of Fear, and education, experience, and personal skill are matters of secondary importance. [4]

In times of great hardship, it is easy to become discouraged and allow our mind to be consumed by fears, worries, and doubts. The challenge is all the greater when we are surrounded by societal noise that feeds off of, and thus nurtures, panic and passivity. Noise from the media, naysayers, and even our well-meaning loved ones can distract us from our purpose, cause us to question our capabilities and distrust our intuition, and overwhelm us into inaction. When we are constantly bombarded by negativity, we feel helpless, and our helplessness translates into a vicious cycle of worst-case thinking. When this happens, our mind—the most important resource we have as human beings—works against us. If we take control of our thoughts, we can take control of our lives and become the "master of [our] fate," as the famous William Ernest Henley poem says.[5]

Seizing control of our thoughts begins with reframing our perspective on adversity, as we will explore in depth in Chapter 2. Failure typically occurs for no reason other than that people quit when they meet with temporary defeat. As Hill explains, "no one is defeated until defeat has been accepted as a reality."[6] Defeat, in the form of derailed plans, disguises itself as failure and settles in the minds of those who lack self-confidence and faith as something final, not to be overcome. However, true greatness is on the other side of temporary defeat. Those who make it to the other side know that nothing compares to the strength, ingenuity, and resolve that come from weathering adversity. Hill's research uncovered this fact: "More than five hundred of the most successful men [America] has ever known, told the author their greatest success came just one step *beyond* the point at which defeat had overtaken them."[7] This book will help you conquer your fears so that you can make it to the other side of failure.

> True greatness is on the other side of temporary defeat.

THREE FEET FROM GOLD: A PARABLE ABOUT "STICKABILITY"

In *Think and Grow Rich*, Hill tells the story of R. U. Darby, a gold prospector who stopped three feet from riches, to illustrate the value of what he calls "stickability"—the ability to persist in one's aims despite challenges.

Darby's uncle went out west during the gold rush and found gold. Lacking the machinery to mine it, he enjoined Darby to raise funds from their relatives and neighbors. After securing the money and purchasing the necessary equipment, Darby and his uncle returned to the mine and drilled an entire car's worth of gold. However, as they continued drilling, they were unable to locate any more ore. Feeling defeated, Darby and his uncle sold the machinery to a junkman for a few hundred dollars.

The junkman hired a mining engineer, who assessed the site and informed the junkman that the previous miners had failed because they did not understand that gold veins often form along fault lines. The junkman discovered that the vein of gold the Darbys had originally tapped was just *three feet* from where they had stopped drilling. Because he was not discouraged by defeat and instead sought the counsel of an expert, the new owner ended up discovering millions of dollars in gold ore.

Rather than wallowing in his ill fate, Darby used it to drive his success in the life insurance industry. He realized that the real source of wealth is one's thoughts, which must be characterized by persistence, desire, and definiteness of purpose. Darby repaid all his debts to his original creditors and sold millions of dollars' worth of life insurance every year. He discovered what Hill's interviewees already had: that phenomenal success often comes only one step *beyond* the point at which defeat overtakes you.

With this story in mind, recognize the incredible power of the human mind to reframe the messaging we are receiving and returning to the universe. As we will explore in the next chapter, not only does this reframing enable us to regain focus, but it also allows us to use the Law of Attraction to our advantage: emitting positive vibrations in the form of constructive thoughts attracts opportunities toward us and mobilizes our subconscious to work in conjunction with our imagination and Infinite Intelligence (Hill's term for the creative force controlling the universe) to identify a definite plan of action for translating our desires into reality.

Failure does not have to be final. Even though Darby initially submitted to defeat, he was able to reset his perspective and become an immensely successful insurance salesman. There is no trouble too great to justify folding to circumstance. Harness the power of your thoughts to begin actively building the life of success you envision for yourself, *even when the time does not seem favorable to such attempts*. In the thick of the Great Depression, Hill recognized the greatness in store for individuals and organizations who could "pivot," exclaiming:

> Never...has there been so great an opportunity for practical dreamers as now exists.... A new race is about to be run. The stakes represent huge fortunes which will be accumulated within the next ten years.[8]

UNPRECEDENTED TIMES

Bearing the subtitle "For men and women who resent poverty," the original 1937 edition of *Think and Grow Rich* discloses its motives: Hill wrote it to help men and women succeed in the face of difficult circumstances, particularly those brought on by the Great Depression. By sharing the achievement principles that had built the fortunes of America's self-made millionaires, he believed that any person—regardless of their level of education or experience—could identify their definite major purpose and use it to attain great wealth. He writes:

> This message is going out to the world at the end of the longest, and perhaps, the most devastating depression America has ever known. It is reasonable to presume that the message may come to the attention of many who have been wounded by the depression, those who have lost their fortunes, others who have lost their positions, and great numbers who must reorganize their plans and stage a comeback. To all these I wish to convey the thought that all achievement, no matter what may be its nature, or its purpose, must begin with an intense, BURNING DESIRE for something definite.[9]

If you are experiencing a difficult time, it might seem impossible to bring yourself to a place of hope. And to that Hill would say—*you shouldn't*. Hoping and wishing are indicative of a lack of faith and inaction. Instead, you should refocus your thoughts on the certainty that you will rebound and achieve your definite chief aim. All you need are new plans, which you can conceive by visualizing the fruition of your desires and instructing your subconscious to find a means for claiming what has already been made available to you. Understand that everything you want most in life is yours for the taking; you are being held back only by your fears, indecision, and lack of proper plans for obtaining what you desire.

There are amazing opportunities found within challenging times—you simply have to open your mind and enlarge your perspective so that you can recognize them. Circumstances that have caused the common person to retreat have launched the world's greatest individuals to the heights of prominence. Hill asserts that

> when a great crisis comes over the world, there always comes out some unknown with a formula for dissolving that crisis—like Abraham Lincoln, for instance, in a time of need, when this country was about to be split asunder by internal strife; by George Washington, preceding Lincoln; by Franklin D. Roosevelt, at a time when the people were stampeded with fear and they were standing in great lines to draw their money out of the bank.[10]

> Circumstances that have caused the common person to retreat have launched the world's greatest individuals to the heights of prominence.

We remember these individuals because they did not let fear sway them from their definite major purpose. In fact, they recognized that the trials they faced were really opportunities in disguise. Rather than giving in to feelings of helplessness, uncertainty, overwhelm, and fear, they changed the channel to which their thoughts were tuned and, by so doing, changed their perspective.

MEET YOUR "OTHER SELF"

Obstacles not only present opportunities in the form of practical plans; they also offer opportunities to build resolve and acquire personal strength. These opportunities occur in the most profound manner when we meet what Hill calls our "other self." Within each person, Hill conjectures, lies two beings:

"

One is a negative sort of person who thinks and moves and lives in an atmosphere of fear and doubt and poverty and ill health. This self expects failure, and seldom is disappointed. It thinks of the circumstances of life which you do not want but which you seem forced to accept—poverty, greed, superstition, fear, doubt, worry and physical sickness.

And one is your "other self," a positive sort of person who thinks in terms of opulence, sound health, love and friendship, personal achievement, creative vision, service to others, and who guides you unerringly to the attainment of all of these blessings.[11]

"

When you confront your other self during a time of crisis, it often marks a turning point in your life: discovering your remarkable ability to transform your strongest emotions into constructive beliefs changes the dynamic of your success journey entirely. Fear, stress, uncertainty—these emotions, when recognized as such, can fuel your achievement. Writing to those who had just weathered the Great Depression, Hill says:

> You have been disappointed, you have undergone defeat during the depression, you have felt the great heart within you crushed until it bled. Take courage, for these experiences have tempered the spiritual metal of which you are made—they are assets of incomparable value.
>
> Remember, too, that all who succeed in life get off to a bad start, and pass through many heart-breaking struggles before they "arrive." The turning point in the lives of those who succeed, usually comes at the moment of some crisis, through which they are introduced to their "other selves."[12]

If you are beset by challenges, this is your time to make your mark on the world. Break through the noise and peel back the layers of your being to find your "other self," which is waiting in expectation for the success and joy in store for you. It is only when you are in a positive and self-confident state of mind that you will receive the means of translating your desires into reality. Fear robs you of these opportunities by derailing your mindset.

> Fear robs you of opportunities by derailing your mindset.

Remember, what separates the individuals with great success stories from those who fall into obscurity is the way they respond to adversity. Will you use the fears and challenges you face to provide greater momentum toward actualizing your dreams, or will you let them drag you backwards? Now is the time for you take courage and not back down. After all, "this changed world requires practical dreamers who can, *and will* put their dreams into action."[13]

It's your time to show the world what you are made of. You have arrived at your turning point.

CLAIM YOUR
COURAGE

Unlearn helplessness by cultivating definiteness of purpose and plans. For example:

- If you feel helpless to obtain a job, build your résumé and network by seeking opportunities for training and mentorship from experts in your desired field.

- If you feel helpless to take control over your health, create a plan to make daily choices about water intake, nutritious eating, and exercise that build incrementally.

- If you feel helpless to mend a broken relationship, request a meeting with the individual and ask for insight into how you can best restore the relationship.

1. Think about those individuals whose success you resent or covet. What do you think is the true source of the negative emotions? Are these individuals living out their calling in a way that you have hindered yourself from doing?

_____

_____

_____

_____

_____

_____

_____

_____

_____

_____

_____

_____

_____

_____

2. What negative influences do you need to eliminate from your environment? Who and/or what inspires doubt, discouragement, fear, and worst-case thinking in you? How can you surround yourself by positive influences that encourage a mindset of confidence and perseverance?

CHAPTER 2

FINDING OPPORTUNITY
WITHIN TEMPORARY DEFEAT

Every failure brings with it the seed of an equivalent advantage.

—**Napoleon Hill,** *Think and Grow Rich*

THE previous chapter emphasized the importance of your state of mind in determining whether fear fuels—or derails—your success journey. This chapter delves deeper into the psychology of success so that you can build the faith and self-confidence you need to vanquish the ghosts of fear that prevent you from wholeheartedly pursuing your dreams, whether they entail material riches, professional accomplishment, intellectual development, or relational happiness. When you can recognize that every obstacle provides an opportunity for personal and professional growth, then all adversity becomes advantageous. That mental shift is one toward success consciousness, and it is the perspective you need to recognize the opportunities that the universe sends your way, particularly during difficult times.

THE SEED IN THE STORM

Hill describes his achievement philosophy as "the art of converting defeat into stepping stones of opportunity."[1] He explains that opportunity "has the sly habit of slipping in by the back door, and often it comes disguised in the form of misfortune, or temporary defeat. Perhaps," he notes, "this is why so many fail to recognize opportunity."[2]

When most people experience adversity, they allow their dominating thoughts to be characterized by fear, fatalism, and self-pity. They focus on the negative, which in turn heightens the negative elements of their life, invites more problems, and inhibits their progress toward their definite chief aim. This is a mindset known as failure consciousness, and it is the surest route to lasting defeat. By focusing on our perceived limitations and obstacles, our subconscious works silently and consistently to ensure that those constraints materialize in our lives.

Hill offers the following crucial advice for shifting our perspective:

> There is no doubt that each of you will experience disappointments and temporary setbacks. And there's no doubt either that collective tragedy—possibly in the form of war or depression—will afflict your generation as it did those that went before you.
>
> But here I can offer you another truth from the science of personal achievement that was my pleasure to formulate during the past fifty years: that is, that every adversity carries with it the seed of an equivalent benefit. Let me repeat that: *Every adversity carries with it the seed of an equivalent benefit.*[3]

All individuals who have reached the apex of success have met with some form of temporary defeat, but they have stayed in the game long enough to find the silver lining to adversity. They recognize that fear and frustration do not have to be destructive; if channeled appropriately, they can fuel one's success journey. As an article in the *Harvard Business Review* states, "For entrepreneurs"—and, Hill would add, for all practical dreamers—"courage is not the absence of fear, but the ability to persist in spite of it."[4]

One such individual is Alexander Graham Bell, inventor of the telephone. In 1857, Bell was experimenting with repurposing a machine called the phonautograph to revolutionize instruction in standard English for deaf speakers. While his "ear phonautograph" did not accomplish its desired aim as an educational resource, it paved the way for the creation of the telephone, as it enabled him to comprehend the ear's tympanic mechanism and construct a sound technology that mirrored it. One small setback led to one of the most significant inventions of the modern world. Imagine if Bell had discontinued his sonic experimentation because his speech-writing device had fallen short of its goal!

Michael Jordan similarly illustrates that defeat can be a source for greater success—an opportunity to distinguish yourself through grit and originality. The inimitable basketball player did not make the cut for his varsity team as a sophomore in high school. Rather than view his defeat as final, he worked tirelessly on developing his skills while on the junior varsity team. Not only did he make the varsity team the next year, but he went on to become one of the greatest basketball players of all time. What is more, by periodically closing his eyes to envision the varsity roster without his name on it, he used his fear to fuel his motivation to out-practice and out-perform the other players. Yet again we see that success is often on the other side of fear...and failure. For "every failure brings with it the seed of an equivalent success."[5]

Even the Great Depression, in Hill's mind, was a boon for those with an entrepreneurial spirit and a positive mental attitude. In many ways, it leveled the playing field, resetting the odds that any one person would achieve success. As Hill writes, "The 'depression' was a blessing in disguise. It reduced the whole world to a new starting point that gives every one a new opportunity."[6] Hill's use of scare quotes around the word "depression" demonstrates that even profound adversity can be reinterpreted as an opportunity for progress. In the thick of challenges, we can choose to surrender or to pivot. But in order to move from a position of fear and failure to one of good fortune, one crucial ingredient is needed: *faith*.

> In the thick of challenges, we can choose to surrender or to pivot.

FAITH

Faith protects the mind from the destructive effects of fear. As Hellen Keller said, "Active faith knows no fear.... It denies despair."[7] When you meet with temporary defeat—and make no mistake, if you are doing anything worthwhile, you will encounter this—you must choose between faith and fear, for they cannot inhabit the mind at the same time. As Hill explains:

> The emergencies of life often bring men to the crossroads, where they are forced to choose their direction, one road being marked Faith and another Fear!
>
> What is it that causes the vast majority to take the Fear road? The choice hinges upon one's *mental attitude*!
>
> The man who takes the Faith road is the man who has conditioned his mind to believe; conditioned it little at a time, by prompt and courageous decisions in the details of his daily experiences. The man who takes the Fear road does so because he has neglected to condition his mind to be positive.[8]

You have a choice over whether you allow fear to write your story or whether you put in the work to actively build faith. While some people may be more predisposed toward positive thinking and self-confidence, there is no human being on this earth who does not have to reinforce their positive beliefs with affirming internal dialogue. There is too much noise, both internal and external, not to filter the sensory input that enters our conscious mind before it reaches our subconscious, where those thoughts become the blueprint for our actions.

When we cultivate an awareness of the negative thoughts that enter our consciousness and the negative emotions that we experience as a result, then we can repurpose them to fuel our success. Unfortunately, as Hill notes, "most people never learn the art of transmuting their strongest emotions into dreams of a constructive nature."[9] Those who distinguish themselves in wealth, influence, or ability recognize negative emotions like fear before they are processed by the subconscious as a blueprint for action (or inaction, as the case may be with fear). We must condition our minds to believe that not only will we receive what we most desire, but that it has already been earmarked for us; all we have to do is identify and implement the practical plans necessary to claim it.

If people confront obstacles with faith instead of fear—if they can use challenges as a means of generating new ideas—then they can achieve more success than they would have been able to under normal circumstances. As Hill asserts, "The whole world ought to know by this time that faith is the starting point of every constructive effort of mankind and that fear is the beginning of most of man's destructive efforts."[10]

Faith accomplishes what material advantages, connections, and education cannot. Hill learned from personal experience the limits of tangible resources like money. When his bank closed its doors during the Depression, he discovered that

"

faith can accomplish that which not all the money in the world can achieve. When I was possessed of all the money I needed, I had made the grievous error of believing money to be power. Now came the astounding revelation that money, without faith, is but so much inert metal, of itself possessed of no power whatsoever.[11]

"

He later adds:

"

My bank has collapsed, but I am still richer than most millionaires because I have faith, and with this I can accumulate other bank accounts and acquire whatever I may need to sustain myself in this maelstrom of activity known as "civilization." Nay, I am richer than most millionaires because I depend upon a source of power that reveals itself to me from within, while they turn for power and stimulation to the stock ticker.[12]

"

Now that you know that the true source of power is not something out of your reach, do not let circumstances serve as an excuse for your fear to keep you down in life. Build your belief in your ability to reach your dreams by using Napoleon Hill's formula for faith. As he exclaims, "FAITH is the only known antidote for FAILURE!"[13]

FORMULA FOR FAITH

1. Not only can I achieve my definite chief aim, but I will achieve it, so I promise to take consistent action to attain it.

2. Acknowledging that my dominant thoughts will become reality, I commit to focusing 30 minutes each day on a clear mental picture of who I most want to become and what my life looks like when I have achieved this desire.

3. Recognizing that whatever desire I focus upon will seek expression in physical form, I will spend 10 minutes every day insisting to my subconscious that I am self-confident.

4. Having written down my definite chief aim in life, I promise myself that I will never stop trying to achieve it.

5. I commit to basing all my efforts in a love of humanity and an intolerance for the lower emotions such as hatred, envy, jealousy, selfishness, and cynicism. I will decline any opportunity that does not benefit all parties involved, realizing that service to others is the surest way to build allies and attain success.

When repeated out loud once a day, this formula can bring you great prosperity, peace of mind, and other invaluable riches, but it also brings a far greater wealth—the certain knowledge that adversity is advantageous when viewed rightly.

> Adversity is advantageous when viewed rightly.

CLAIM YOUR
COURAGE

Master the fear of failure by finding opportunity within adversity. For example:

- If your sales pitch is rejected, ask what you can learn from it. Answer the following questions: Why didn't they choose you or your product? What are follow-up questions you could ask them—or even yourself—to learn from your rejection? How can you grow from it? What other doors might be opened because of this rejection?

- If you lose your job, consider what better opportunity awaits you. What other position might you find that gives you more freedom, more income, and/or more time with your family? Can you finally make a career change that you've been longing to make?

- If you experience a financial setback, use it as an opportunity to make a financial plan so that your security isn't dependent on what life will throw your way. Also, consider what additional opportunities are available to you to earn extra income.

Use the table below to identify the seeds of opportunity that might be found in the pockets of adversity in your life. In the left-hand column, write a list of all the challenges you are currently facing, including fears that are holding you back from acting on your dreams. In the right-hand column, brainstorm opportunities that might be found within each of these obstacles.

Challenges	Opportunities

CHAPTER 3

FEARENZA AND WORRYITIS

Without doubt, the most common weakness of all human beings is the habit of leaving their minds open to the negative influence of other people.

—**Napoleon Hill,** *Think and Grow Rich*

FEAR defeats more people than any other thing in the world."[1] The ability to deflate this force can, and often does, mean the difference between success and failure, happiness and misery.

"Fearenza," so called by Hill in *Think and Grow Rich*, is a virus that is fatal to sucess: it multiplies within an individual until it destroys his or her organs of creativity and industry. Its toxic effects are not confined to its host: it is remarkably contagious, spreading its poison from person to person. Once in the grip of fear, it can be extremely difficult to extricate oneself because it requires identifying and uprooting the misconceptions that have embedded themselves in one's subconscious and, in the process, shrouded themselves in a general haze of worry.

When those who meet with temporary defeat respond with fear, the results can be quite disastrous—especially when the response is widespread. For Hill, this is what exacerbated the negative consequences of the Great Depression. As he writes, "The whole world has had ample opportunity, during the recent business depression, to witness what the LACK OF FAITH will do to business."[2] He continues: there is "evidence in abudance that widespread FEAR will paralyze the wheels of industry and business."[3] Fear can grind an entire economy to a halt, destroying the livelihoods of millions of people and their belief in themselves.

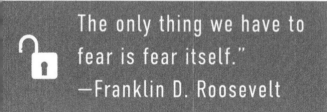

The only thing we have to fear is fear itself."
—Franklin D. Roosevelt

Recognizing that this negative emotion was responsible for fanning the flames of financial hysteria during the Depression, Hill gave Franklin D. Roosevelt the idea for the famous line in his inaugural address: "The only thing we have to fear is fear itself."[4] Indeed, it is so insidious that Hill lists "Freedom from Fear" as the fourth of the Twelve Riches of Life. He reasons:

> No man who fears anything is a free man! Fear is a harbinger of evil, and wherever it appears one may find a cause which must be eliminated before he may become rich in the fuller sense.[5]

But do not despair—there is a cure for this disease, one that will be explored in the next chapter. First we must demystify the seven primary fears and an eighth saboteur so malicious that Hill refers to it as an "evil."

WHEN VULNERABILITY IS DANGEROUS

Over the course of his studies, Hill identifies a natural force that makes thought habits, including fear-based ones, extraordinarily powerful:

> What strange fear is it that gets into the minds of men and short-circuits their approach to this secret power from within, and when it is recognized and used lifts men to great heights of achievement? How and why do the vast majority of the people of the world become the victims of a hypnotic rhythm which destroys their capacity to use the secret power of their own minds? How can this rhythm be broken?[6]

What Hill is referring to here is what he calls "Cosmic Habit-force"—the force that can work either for good or for bad depending on whether the thoughts it replicates are constructive or destructive. Because of the incredible power of the subconscious to work for or against us in materializing our dominating thoughts (whether voluntary or involuntary), the greatest "evil" we face as humans—something more harmful than any of the six basic fears—is our *susceptibility to negative influences*. To underscore the epigraph that opens this chapter: "Without doubt, the most common weakness of all human beings is the habit of leaving their minds open to the negative influence of other people."[7] Our vulnerability to others' negativity and misguided ideas effects the same results as hypnosis: we become lulled into a state of helplessness and self-destructive behavior, whether in the form of inaction or frenzy. This allows destructive thoughts to embed themselves into our subconscious and work in tandem with it to become reality.

In order to combat this harmful tendency, you must develop your reserve of willpower, building a fortress around your subconscious mind and filtering out any destructive messages before they take root in it. This shortcoming is tremendously difficult to acknowledge, Hill notes, because most people are not aware that they are under the influence of others, and when they do recognize it they often refuse to address it. Recognize that you are the most susceptible to negative influences that harmonize with your weaknesses. For example, if you already fear risk-taking, then you will be more easily swayed by messages that play into this fear. Knowing this about yourself can help you more critically approach messages that reinforce a fear of risk-taking, testing out their truthfulness before you accept them without hesitation.

Secondly, you should avoid negative people and keep company only with supportive individuals who encourage you to think and act for yourself. As is often said, you are the average of the five people with whom you spend the most time. By extension, if you spend the majority of your days with people who subscribe to negativity and media-induced frenzy, then you will likely become an agent of this panic yourself. (This is also why it is crucial to choose your spouse carefully.) Our susceptibility to negative influences causes us to become subject to the control of outside forces, reducing us to mere mediums for propaganda. When ignored, this tendency shackles us, forcing us to be prisoners to fear. When exposed, it can be countered by building a wall of immunity in the mind. Take the assessment at the end of the book to determine how susceptible you really are to the negative influences of others, and use the results to help you establish boundaries to protect your mental attitude and the trajectory your life takes.

THE SEVEN GHOSTS OF FEAR

"Every human being has the ability to completely control his own mind."[8] To become the master of your fate and harness the immense power of your mind to create the life of your dreams, you must first understand yourself, recognizing which of the seven basic fears you are the most susceptible to. If any of these negative influences are operating on your subconscious, then what Hill terms your "Sixth Sense"—your creative imagination, which generates concrete plans for the attainment of your desires—cannot function properly. In other words, fear is a state of mind that inhibits the part of our brain responsible for inspiration. When we are controlled by fear, our perspective is too limited to see the opportunities that are all around us. We must disempower the ghosts of fear by naming them and recognizing that they are unreliable emotions, not facts upon which to stake our future. The following are the seven most common fears, into which all other fears can be grouped:

- Fear of poverty
- Fear of criticism
- Fear of ill health
- Fear of loss of love
- Fear of loss of liberty[9]
- Fear of old age
- Fear of death

> Fears are unreliable emotions, not facts upon which to stake our future.

1. FEAR OF POVERTY

The fear of poverty is the most destructive of all the seven basic fears because it is the most difficult to master. It has become ingrained in human nature owing to our tendency to take advantage of others for our own economic gain as well as our awareness of the suffering that poverty entails, including the damage it causes to our ego. Of this fear, Hill writes:

> This fear paralyzes the faculty of reason, destroys the faculty of imagination, kills off self-reliance, undermines enthusiasm, discourages initiative, leads to uncertainty of purpose, encourages procrastination...and makes self-control an impossibility. It takes the charm from one's personality, destroys the possibility of accurate thinking, diverts concentration of effort, it masters persistence, turns will-power into nothingness, destroys ambition, beclouds the memory and invites failure in every conceivable form...all this despite the obvious truth that we live in a world of over-abundance of everything the heart could desire, with nothing standing between us and our desires, excepting lack of a definite purpose.[10]

The most common symptoms of the fear of poverty are as follows: the lack of ambition, the inability to think for oneself, using doubt to make excuses for one's failures, self-destructive behavior in the form of overspending and intemperance, regular criticism of others, and overcautiousness that leads to inaction. Fearing poverty, we fail to pursue business opportunities or otherwise follow our dreams. We become so consumed with our perceived lack of financial resources that our resentment eats away at our originality, accountability, and persistence. We waste time obsessing over our bank balance instead of developing a plan for building wealth. In our idleness, we scowl at those who have become successful after mastering this fear through calculated risk-taking and develop a negative personality characterized by miserliness and bitterness or, alternatively, intemperance and indifference.

We can see the disastrous effects of this fear in the public's response to the Wall Street crash of 1929—a response that intensified the economic crisis until it became a depression. Hill explains:

"

The people of America began to think of poverty, following the Wall Street crash of 1929. Slowly, but surely that mass thought was crystallized into its physical equivalent, which was known as a 'depression.' This had to happen, it is in conformity with the laws of Nature.[11]

Why did natural law dictate that widespread fear of poverty must materialize as an economic depression? It is the same reason that autosuggestion, or the repetition of emotionalized thoughts to program the subconcious, is so powerful: "all thought has a tendency to clothe itself in its physical equivalent."[12] The fear of poverty can never translate into financial gain—only economic hardship and limitation.

DO YOU FEAR POVERTY OR LOSS
OF FINANCIAL WELL-BEING?

1. Is the fear of poverty holding you back because you value things more than you value freedom of thought and time?

_____

_____

_____

_____

2. Are you failing to pursue your dreams or explore business opportunities because you worry about losing money?

_____

_____

_____

_____

Now is the perfect time to create a financial plan so that you can conquer the fear of poverty through organized planning!

2. FEAR OF CRITICISM

Look around at everyone's heavily curated social media feeds and use of the Internet as an echo chamber, and you will see just how commonplace the fear of criticism has become in today's world. Hill attributes its origins to the human tendency to justify egregious actions toward others by attacking their character—in other words, to build ourselves up by tearing others down. This fear is responsible for people-pleasing tendencies, the compulsion to "keep up with the Joneses," and the uncritical acceptance of doctrine and dominant narratives. We sabotage ourselves out of concern that our risk will be met with negative feedback or laughter, particularly from our loved ones. This fear roots itself more deeply in individuals whose parents were highly critical of them as children, causing them to develop an inferiority complex. Parents and other mentors should note that criticism sows only fear and resentment, whereas love and constructive feedback yield a genuine desire for self-improvement that is grounded in the realization of one's worth.

When this fear becomes more developed, it diminishes one's creativity, destroys one's ability to think for oneself, and weakens one's initiative. Symptoms include *self-consciousness*, often manifesting as social awkwardness and shyness; *indecision*, particularly in forming and expressing firm positions on important issues; *a sense of inferiority* masked by a heightened attention to personal appearance; *extravagance* intended to "keep up with the Joneses"; *lack of initiative* manifesting as procrastination; and *lack of ambition*, resulting from concern that any bold moves will bring criticism.

DO YOU FEAR CRITICISM OR
LACK OF ACCEPTANCE?

1. Do you ask for—and accept—constructive criticism? How can you be bolder in seeking feedback in order to overcome the fear of criticism? Once you receive this feedback, how can you evaluate its usefulness without sacrificing your certainty in your definite major purpose?

_____

_____

_____

_____

2. How do you engage in people-pleasing tendencies? How can you overcome these tendencies by creating your lifestyle according to your own wants and desires? How can contentment serve as a weapon to wield against the urge to "keep up with the Joneses"?

_____

_____

_____

_____

Now is the perfect time to establish your values so that you can defeat the fear of criticism and build a lifestyle and career that are authentic to you!

3. FEAR OF ILL HEALTH

This fear, like the fear of old age and the fear of death, is always present at some level, insofar as humans do not like to face their own mortality and develop neuroses when they focus too much on it. Because our subconscious works on material-izing our thought impulses—especially ones that are heavily emotionalized—"the fear of disease...often produces the phys-ical symptoms of the disease feared."[13] Its other effects include the following: *addiction to health fads*; *hypochondria*; *weakened immune system*, caused by the mind working to create favorable conditions for the disease; *self-indulgence*, or using a perceived or expected illness as an excuse for failure or lack of ambition; and *intemperance*, resulting from an attempt to use alcohol and other narcotics as a means of combating the unpleasant symptoms of ill health rather than the root causes.

Panic is, by its very definition, fear that has moved from constructive to destructive— controlled to frenzied.

As we have seen, the fear of ill health reaches epic proportions during times of pandemic, sending people to the stores in droves to empty the shelves of toilet paper, hand sanitizer, and face masks. According to *National Geographic,* this "panic buying" is an evolutionary response intended to induce a sense of control over one's survival.[14] And yet, panic is, by its very definition, fear that has moved from constructive to destructive—controlled to frenzied.

Panic over epidemics occurs thanks in large part to the media, who seizes on the spread of illness as an opportunity to generate revenue by fueling people's fears. Hill recognized this with the Spanish flu outbreak in 1918:

> During the "flu" epidemic which broke out during the world war, the mayor of New York City took drastic steps to check the damage which people were doing themselves through their inherent fear of ill health. He called in the newspaper men and said to them, "Gentlemen, I feel it necessary to ask you not to publish any scare headlines concerning the 'flu' epidemic. Unless you cooperate with me, we will have a situation which we cannot control." The newspapers quit publishing stories about the "flu," and within one month the epidemic had been successfully checked.[15]

Feeding the public horror story after horror story, the media subdues their viewership's reasoning faculties until they become entirely dependent on and addicted the news for an adrenaline rush and justification for their state of indolence. This messaging effectively short-circuits our brains because, when faced with profound uncertainties, our brain protects itself by implementing availability bias: it retrieves and relies on the most accessible information, which is the recurring messages we see in head-lines.[16] Because of this, people would do well to limit the amount of news that they consume during times of pandemic so that they do not let the fear of disease affect their mental health and their ability to carry on with their regular tasks, including the actions they must continue to take in pursuit of their definite chief aim.

DO YOU FEAR ILLNESS?

1. Oftentimes we fear sickness because we recognize that we are not taking care of ourselves the way we should be. How can you carve out more time for self-care—exercise, meditation, relaxation, etc.—to support your mental and physical health?

_____

_____

_____

_____

2. How are superstition and media frenzy perpetuating your fear of ill health? Which health fads or fears are governing the way you live to the point where you have become neurotic?

_____

_____

_____

_____

Now is the perfect time to create a health plan regarding diet, lifestyle, and exercise based on sound medical advice!

4. FEAR OF LOSS OF LOVE

When we fall in love, that love typically is accompanied by a fear that we will lose that person, whether to death or to someone else. In many ways, this fear can be the most debilitating, as it can completely alter our perception of reality, skewing how we process sensory data and impacting our mental health. Its most common symptoms include *jealousy*, or constant, unmerited suspicion; *fault finding*, hypercritical attention directed to everyone, not just one's romantic partner; *extravagance*, used to "buy love"; and *adultery*, or cheating on a partner out of fear that he or she will be unfaithful first. Those who fall prey to this fear often ensure it becomes justified because it poisons the relationship, driving their significant other away from them.

DO YOU FEAR ABANDONMENT
AND LOSS OF LOVE?

1. How are you trying to protect yourself from being hurt by
    pushing others away?

    _____

    _____

    _____

    _____

2. If you focus on loving others rather than on being loved, there
    is less room for jealousy, fault-finding, suspicion, and other
    behaviors that sabotage a relationship. How can you open your
    heart to give more love?

    _____

    _____

    _____

    _____

Now is the perfect time to commit to loving others selflessly and
without hesitation! You'll find that the more love you give, the more
love you'll receive in return.

5. FEAR OF LOSS OF LIBERTY

Human beings value their independence so much that any threat to their freedom provokes a dramatic fight-or-flight response. Fearing our individual rights will be violated, we create discord between ourselves and others with differing political opinions. We treat any dissenting opinion as though it were a personal attack on our very being. We fail to take chances in business and life out of concern that we will lose our economic independence. We avoid the topic of disability or old age for fear of thinking about a life without complete physical independence. This fear infects our professional relationship with our superiors by allowing resentment to fester when we feel like we do not have a voice.

Ultimately, this fear causes us to turn inward out of suspicion that any outsider intends to control us in some way, but in doing so, we give up our control to them. Building walls around ourselves, we miss opportunities that would come by collaboration, compromise, and calculated risk-taking. Common symptoms of this fear include *prejudice/dogmatism*, or narrow-minded views meant to safeguard our worldview; *hoarding*; *paranoia*; *controlling behavior*, e.g., observing strict routines to assert control over one's life; *apathy*, or failure to undertake any definite plan for fear of its economic consequences; and *social isolation*, stemming from an unwillingness or inability to collaborate with others.

DO YOU FEAR THE LOSS OF
YOUR FREEDOM?

1. How can you open your mind to ideas and beliefs that differ from your own?

_____

_____

_____

_____

2. How can you enlarge your perspective by learning to appreciate influences outside your community? Consider how travel can free you from the fear of loss of liberty.

_____

_____

_____

_____

Now is the perfect time to eliminate the fear of loss of freedom by finding security and agency in a diversity of perspectives!

6. FEAR OF OLD AGE

This fear typically grows stronger as we get older. It derives from an association of poverty with old age and concern over what is to come after death. It also emerges out of a suspicion of others who might be seeking an inheritance, concern about the potential for poor health and quality of life, fear of diminished sexual appeal/activity, and concerns about the loss of one's economic and physical freedom. Its more pronounced manifestations can be seen in a *midlife crisis*, or a sudden onset of immaturity in one's "middle years" that results from a fear of having passed one's "best" years; an *inferiority complex*, or thinking one has less value because of one's age; and a *tendency to settle* because one feels it is too late to act on one's dreams. This fear is magnetized by a debilitating nostalgia that can cause one to focus too much on the past, neglecting the future. How much time have we wasted wishing we could relive our youth instead of actively working to create a gratifying future? It is never too late to live your best life.

It is never too late
to live your best life.

DO YOU FEAR OLD AGE?

1. Combat the fear that your "best years" have passed by identifying the fruits of aging. What benefits and joys do you anticipate enjoying as you age? What new freedoms and opportunities will emerge, and how will you gain wisdom?

_____

_____

_____

_____

2. Oftentimes fear results from ignorance. How can you increase your comfort with the aging process by volunteering at a retirement community and/or expanding your mastermind group to include older members?

_____

_____

_____

_____

Now is the perfect time to stop letting the fear of aging prevent you from enjoying your present and planning for your future!

7. FEAR OF DEATH

The fear of death typically results not from a fear of dying, but rather a fear of what the afterlife—or lackthereof, depending on your beliefs—might entail. Visions of hellfire or nothingness cause humans to repress the thought of death. Those who become prey to this fear agonize over potential threats to their survival to the point that they are afraid of living and miss out on their life. Common symptoms include *inaction*, or indecision resulting from a focus on death; *hoarding*, or a fear of poverty and leaving one's family without resources that manifests in the obsessive acquisition of material goods; and *religious fanaticism*, or getting carried away by extreme religious doctrine to make oneself feel better prepared for death.

Hill asserts that the fear of death, if channeled appropriately, can be quite productive: if one can accept death as a reality, the thought can be passed out of one's mind so that one can focus on service to others and attaining one's definite chief aim. For Hill, death is not something to fear because it is just another instance of what he termed "transmutation," or the transfer of energy from one object (animate or inanimate) to another. Following the laws of Nature, death is not a passing away into nothingness, since energy can neither be created nor destroyed; it is simply a transition into another state.

DO YOU FEAR DEATH?

1. Oftentimes we fear death because we worry that we won't have sufficiently "lived" when our time comes. To that end, the best cure for the fear of death is identifying and pursuing your definite major purpose. How can you live according to your life purpose rather than wasting time on things that will matter less in the end?

    _____

    _____

    _____

    _____

2. The fear of death is also exacerbated by a feeling that we are not prepared for death. What relationships do you need to get in order? What financial and end-of-life plans (e.g., life insurance, will, living will, durable power of attorney, etc.) do you need to have drawn up?

    _____

    _____

    _____

    _____

    Now is the perfect time to vanquish the fear of death by building your legacy!

These seven fears—intangible forces that exist only in the mind—wreak more havoc on humankind than any "real" enemy. But it is entirely within an individual's control to regulate his or her mind by weeding out these fears or, alternately, using them to drive one's success, and to admit only constructive impulses of thought.

THE SECONDARY INFECTION OF WORRYITIS

When the pandemic of Fearenza spreads, the result is a secondary condition known as Worryitis. It occurs when a fear has become so embedded in the subconscious that it unsettles the mind, making one feel helpless and unable to make decisions. It destroys self-confidence and reduces an individual's ability to take action on his or her dreams. As Hill explains in *Think and Grow Rich*, worrying produces four negative results:

1. It spreads fear to others.

2. It paralyzes the creative and critical faculties.

3. It embeds a fear into one's subconscious, which works to produce its physical equivalent.

4. It creates a negative, unpleasant personality.

Because we invite into our lives the subject of our dominating thoughts, worry has a tendency to turn our fears into reality. With that in mind, and with a full desire to live in the present, unfettered by the ghosts of fear, we turn next to exploring the cure for these terrible conditions.

CALL TO
COURAGE

Build immunity to the contagions of fear and worry by developing a reserve of willpower. For example:

- If you are particularly susceptible to impulse shopping, a manifestation of the fear of poverty, create a three-day waiting period before purchasing an item. If shopping online, free to add the item to your cart, but wait three full days to complete the purchase. More often than not, you'll discover that the urge to buy the item has passed. Regardless, forcing yourself to wait will help you build willpower and restraint in spending.

- If you struggle with procrastination, another manifestation of the fear of poverty, buy an egg timer and set it for 30-minute intervals. During those 30 minutes, focus exclusively on the most urgent task on your desk. When the timer goes off, you can reset it for a 5-minute mental break, and then repeat the entire process. As you develop your willpower, you will be able to set the egg timer for longer than 30 minutes. Eventually, you may come to see that you do not need the timer to regulate your work habits.

> Worry has a tendency to turn our fears into reality.

Beyond our natural weaknesses, negative influences in our environment can make us more prone to a fear-based mindset. Complete the self-analysis questionnaire provided at the end of this book. Based on your results, how susceptible are you to the negative influences of others? How will you adjust your daily behaviors to better protect yourself from these influences?

_____

_____

_____

_____

_____

_____

_____

_____

_____

_____

_____

CHAPTER 4

ENTERING THE
STREAM OF POWER

Tell the world what you intend to do, but first show it.

—**Napoleon Hill,** Think and Grow Rich

A S we explored in the last chapter, fear makes us prisoners to our emotions. Environmental influences work to strengthen these bonds by exacerbating our fears until they become panic and hysteria. When we are kept in a state of fear, we are innocuous, lacking the drive, creativity, and fortitude to take advantage of opportunities for success. Fear renders us helpless, apathetic, complacent, and worse—sources of contagion who spread fear and worry to others.

But the world does not need people who soak up the noise of society and use it as an excuse to maintain the status quo. It needs pioneers who see challenges as an opportunity to create something new and to render service to others through innovation. As Ralph Waldo Emerson offers, "He has not learned the lesson of life who does not every day surmount a fear."[1] It is time to take back control of your life, step into the stream of power, and use the mind's incredible creative faculties to drive, rather than inhibit, your success.

> The world needs pioneers who find opportunity in adversity, rather than people who use societal noise as an excuse to maintain the status quo.

FROM HABIT TO MINDSET

Although the seven basic fears and the eighth evil can fester and spread undetected in our subconscious, there is a relatively simple cure. According to Hill, the "only known antidote for these germs...is the habit of prompt and firm DECISION."[2]

Because fears work to paralyze us into a state of inaction, the only cure for them is to create momentum in a constructive direction, which requires decisiveness. As Hill explains, "Fear, the worst of all enemies, can be effectively cured by *forced repetition of acts of courage*."[3] Similar to exposure therapy, this treatment breaks the emotional power of the fear by confronting it in stages, with the intention of demonstrating the source's harmlessness.[4] In other words, if you consistently make the decision to act in spite of your fear, that fear will lose its strength as it is replaced by the knowledge of its irrationality and the satisfaction of making progress on your success journey.

> "Most people are the servants, not the masters of their emotions, because they have never established definite, systematic habits of control over them."
>
> **—Napoleon Hill**

Recognize that fear and suspectibility to negative influences are emotional states that have generated a destructive set of habits and, as such, are *completely within our control*. Because of this, we must resolve to make new and better mental habits. As Hill explains, "Every man is a bundle of habits. Some are of his own making while others are involuntary. They are made by his fears and doubts and worries and anxieties and greed and superstition and envy and hatred."[5] We can control and direct our habits of thought, severing the connection between emotion and thought (and, in turn, action). Self-discipline is crucial here: it requires becoming consciously aware of our feelings, including what external and internal messages are contributing to them; neutralizing the emotionalized thought impulses before they penetrate our subconscious; and taking action in the opposite direction that the fear attempts to move you.

For example, when you feel afraid of making a sales call, you might go through the following process: name and acknowledge the feeling and the fear from which it derives (the fear of criticism), take a deep breath and release the emotion as you exhale, replace the destructive thought impulse with a constructive one in the form of an affirmation (e.g., "This opportunity, product, etc., will add significant value to this person's life."), and then act in spite of your fear (e.g., pick up the phone and make the call!).

Depending on which of the fears are most prevalent in your state of mind, you can cater your plan of action accordingly. If, for instance, you struggle with **the fear of poverty**, you can decide to make do with, and be grateful for, the financial resources you presently have, regardless of what they are. You can regulate your spending and saving in a way that gives you peace of mind should you experience a period of financial drought.

Those who wrestle with **the fear of criticism** can be cured by making the decision not to care about what people think, say, or do. Establishing their self-worth, they can resolve to repel the negative words or attitudes of others and to act without that consideration in mind.

The fear of ill health can be cured by committing to take care of the body and mind through proper nutrition, exercise, and self-care, as well as deciding to seek and trust trained medical professionals when one experiences any unusual symptoms.

For those plagued by **the fear of loss of love**, the decision to live a fulfilling, meaningful life with or without a romantic partner can liberate them from its bonds. Learning to find joy in friendships and in the relationship one has with oneself, as well as trusting in the strength of your romantic relationship, will not only liberate you from mental torment, but it will also deepen the bond you share with your partner.

The fear of loss of liberty can be treated through the decision to accept any challenges that come along and exert control over the attitude and determination with which one faces every day. When you have your life under control, it is much easier to resist outside influences without being overly suspicious of others' intentions.

The fear of old age can be cured by deciding to accept the aging process and enjoy the benefits that come with it, including opportunities for wisdom, leisure, and legacy building.

And finally, **the fear of death** can be cured by resolving to accept one's mortality and to live fully in the present, appreciating each day as a chance to enjoy the fruits of love, service, and progress.

> Decide today that nothing is worth the price of worry.

For those whose fears have compounded into a general state of **worry**, the best cure is deciding once and for all that nothing is worth the price of worry. After all, is there anything worse than the perpetual unease and dissatisfaction that worry brings? Indeed, the experience of fear and worry are often more unpleasant than that which we fear itself.

THE RIGHT SIDE OF THE RIVER

Habits propel us in a particular direction because of a natural principle that Hill calls "Cosmic Habitforce." It is the force that supports the functioning of autosuggestion, which is the process of feeding your subconscious voluntary or involuntary thoughts so that it works to materialize them. Thoughts that are magnetized by emotion are more readily received and acted upon by the subconscious. This is why fear can be so destructive: it magnetizes negative thought impulses and enjoins the subconscious to manifest them in reality. In time, these thoughts become fixed as states of mind, which further cements the habits of thought that shifted our perspective to begin with. For instance, the fear of poverty can become fixed as the mindset of poverty consciousness through repeated thoughts about financial loss—a mindset that cannot work constructively to build financial wealth but rather directs the subconscious and Infinite Intelligence to create plans that fulfill the person's negative expectations.

To explain the incredible power of this principle to accelerate our growth or failure, Hill uses the metaphor of the Great

River of Life. As this Great River, Cosmic Habitforce has both a positive and a negative potentiality—two streams that flow in opposite directions:

> There exists a great unseen stream of POWER, which may be compared to a river; except that one side flows in one direction, carrying all who get into that side of the stream, onward and upward to WEALTH—and the other side flows in the opposite direction, carrying all who are unfortunate enough to get into it (and not able to extricate themselves from it), downward to misery and POVERTY.[6]

Using the principles described above to filter out negative thought impulses and replace them with constructive ones, magnetized by positive emotions such as faith and love, will place you on the side of the river that brings success, however you define it. As Hill details:

"

You can make your thought habits to order and they will carry you to the attainment of any desired goal within your reach. Or you can allow the uncontrollable circumstances of your life to make your thought habits for you and they will carry you irresistibly into the failure side of the great River of Life.

You can keep your mind trained on that which you desire from Life and get just that! Or you can feed it on thoughts of that which you do not desire and it will, as unerringly, bring you just that. *Your thought habits evolve from the food that your mind dwells upon.*[7]

"

It is completely within your power to conquer the ghosts of fear, protect yourself from the negative influences of others, and create thought habits that prime you for great success and profound, lasting fulfillment.

"

Turn on the full powers of your will and take complete control of your own mind. It is your mind! It was given to you as a servant to carry out your desires. And no one may enter it or influence it in the slightest degree *without your consent and cooperation.*[8]

"

CALL TO
COURAGE

Break the emotional power of fear by disentangling thoughts and actions from the negative emotions motivating them. For example:

- If you respond to conflict by yelling, you might really be experiencing the fear of loss of liberty, which causes you to feel threatened when someone disagrees with you.

- If you quit at the first sign of defeat—like if you prematurely discard a business plan because you fail to attract clients in the first month—you might really be experiencing the fear of poverty and the fear of criticism, which cause you to feel anxious about and embarassed by slow progress.

- If you are experiencing a mid-career malaise, you might really be suffering from the fear of old age, which can lead to feelings of inferiority.

Cultivate an awareness of your thought habits by recording them for a week. Determine which ones are constructive and which ones are destructive. For each destructive thought impulse, identify the larger fear or negative emotion that is magnetizing it and make a decision to act (constructively) in opposition of the feeling.

Day	Thought	Constructive or Destructive?	Fear or Emotion	Faith-Based Action

1. What new thoughts and behaviors can you implement to solicit Cosmic Habitforce to work in your favor, translating constructive thought habits into positive states of mind?

---

2. Record your progress, noting in particular any changes in your overall mindset and new opportunities that you are able to identify.

_____

_____

_____

_____

_____

_____

_____

_____

_____

_____

_____

_____

_____

_____

CHAPTER 5

THE METTLE
IN THE MASTERMIND

When a man becomes the master of his own
emotions, and learns the blessed art of self-
expression through useful service to others, he has
gone far toward the development of a Positive Mental
Attitude.

—**Napoleon Hill,** The Master-Key to Riches

I is entirely within every individual's power to control his or her thoughts and emotions, but this process can be greatly supported by the mastermind principle. Hill defines a mastermind as "an alliance of two or more minds, blended in a spirit of perfect harmony and cooperating for the attainment of a definite purpose."[1] By virtue of this alliance, individuals may "absorb power directly from the great universal storehouse of Infinite Intelligence," which stimulates the mind to operate at a higher frequency of thought within a framework of faith, the most powerful positive emotion.[2]

> Peace of mind is the ultimate form of wealth that pays endless dividends.

When you form a partnership with individuals whose expertise and experience complement (not replicate) your own, you can greatly enhance your Sixth Sense, the creative imagination, which is the source of inspiration. As Hill explains, "Every human brain is both a broadcasting station and a receiving station for the expression of vibrations of thought, and the stimulating effect of the Master Mind principle stimulates action of thought."[3] This occurs in two primary ways: one, through the exchange of ideas during regular meetings; and two, through the "third mind" that is formed from the network of thought impulses generated by the mastermind alliance. Indeed, simply by jointly focusing on a shared definite chief aim, the group's thought vibrations can become magnified to such an extent that the alliance will access a higher plane of thinking and generate original ideas. With the help of a mastermind, individuals can overcome destructive states of mind such as fear and worry and use challenges as motivation to innovate and create. They can obtain the ultimate form of wealth that pays endless dividends: *peace of mind.*

PROSPERITY THROUGH PARTNERSHIP

Hill recognized that difficult circumstances hold the potential for individual and societal transformation, particularly when experienced on a mass scale. This transformation can be constructive or destructive, depending on how people respond to temporary defeat. During times of depression and world war, for instance, Hill identifies how:

> A new spirit is sweeping the world in spite of the dark fears raised by the threat of nuclear warfare. Man is indeed learning that he is his brother's keeper! ... Never in the history of mankind have so many persons devoted their time and energy and wealth to helping other men and women.[4]

Difficult times and shared anxieties offer the perfect opportunity to implement the mastermind principle. When people combine their skills and knowledge to "pivot" and innovate, they can create opportunities for themselves and others and address unmet needs. For this reason, the most effective cure for Fearenza and Worryitis is *service*.

> The best cure for Fearenza and Worryitis is *service*.

When people focus on adding value to others, it is nearly impossible to be consumed by fear and other negative emotions. As Hill says, "Positive and negative emotions cannot occupy the mind at the same time."[5] Simply by engaging in service, individuals can amplify the positive emotions of faith, love, hope, and charity, spreading constructive thought impulses to others as well as cultivating a positive state of mind themselves, which, in turn, yields prosperity.

If you are suffering from the fear of poverty, consider how you might feel richer through the act of giving. In your mastermind group, work together to identify a way to add value to others' lives that might have the secondary benefit of profit. Can you serve your customers in a new way? Create a product to meet an unfulfilled need?

If you are suffering from the fear of criticism, shower others with compliments. In your mastermind group, reflect on a way to build others up through service or innovation. Is there a community (virtual or otherwise) that you could create to support others' personal growth? An edifying book you could write? A product that would help people feel better about themselves?

If you are suffering from the fear of ill health, volunteer at a hospital or bring homemade meals to someone who is sick. In your mastermind group, collaborate to identify a means of helping people support their mental and physical health.

If you are suffering from the fear of loss of love, share your love with others. In your mastermind group, help members strengthen their relationships by encouraging each other to be the best partners they can be.

If you are suffering from the fear of loss of liberty, volunteer at a prison or work to help others protect their freedoms. In your mastermind group, reflect on a way to liberate people from something that is limiting their freedom, whether it is something that is infringing on their family time or restricting their access to needed resources.

If you are suffering from the fear of old age, volunteer at a retirement community. In your mastermind group, jointly consider how the wisdom and experience of each group member could help others who are just beginning their success journeys. Find opportunities for mentorship.

If you are suffering from the fear of death, determine how to help people live more fully in the present. In your mastermind group, discuss ways that each member can build a lasting legacy.

Fear might feel like an isolating experience, but when we partner with others to channel our concerns in productive directions, we can find new pathways for prosperity and growth that improve others' lives as well as our own. And because we can better combat the indecision and doubt that fear inspires in a mastermind group, we can bring these ideas to life by creating and implementing a definite plan of action.

> Fear, properly channeled, can help us discover new pathways for prosperity and growth.

Do not allow fear to write your story. You have control over your emotions and your response to temporary defeat! Enlarge your perspective by having faith in your ability to attain your definite chief aim and you will discover countless opportunities awaiting your initiative.

It is time to master your emotions...and by extension, your life.

It is time to become the trailblazer you were meant to be.

Harness the power of your thoughts to trade fear for fortitude.

Take courage, and take action on your dreams.

> Never has there been a time more favorable to pioneers than the present.[6]

CALL TO
COURAGE

Pivot by converting shared anxieties and difficult circumstances into opportunities for service. For example:

- If your business is slowing down, partner with other nearby companies to host a fundraiser or offer a package of services/products where a percentage of the proceeds benefits a local nonprofit.

- If you have experienced the loss of a loved one, honor their memory by helping other people through the grieving process, either by facilitating a support group or offering other resources helpful to those in a similar situation.

Form a mastermind group to help you overcome your most pronounced fear by determining how best to add value to others.

1. Most powerful or most disruptive fear:

_____

_____

_____

_____

_____

_____

_____

_____

_____

_____

_____

_____

_____

_____

_____

_____

_____

2. Individuals who could provide the experience, training, education, specialized knowledge, and/or talent you need to redirect this fear toward a productive end:

1. _____

2. _____

3. _____

4. _____

5. _____

6. _____

7. _____

8. _____

9. _____

10. _____

3. How can these potential mastermind members support you in converting fear into opportunity?

_____

_____

_____

_____

_____

_____

_____

_____

_____

_____

_____

_____

_____

_____

_____

_____

4. How can you contribute value to them?

5. Target date to begin discussions with mastermind:

   _____

6. Commit now to contacting these potential mastermind members and forming an alliance of individuals who will encourage you to conquer your fears and innovate in times of adversity. Meet with them weekly. Record the ideas that emerge out of your brainstorming sessions, periodically reflecting on the evolution of your own mental attitude.

   _____

   _____

   _____

   _____

   _____

   _____

   _____

   _____

   _____

   _____

   _____

CHAPTER 6

THIS CHANGING WORLD AND FAITH[1]

FAITH permits one to approach within communicating distance of Infinite Intelligence (or God, if you prefer that name). Fear holds one at arm's length and makes communication impossible.

Faith creates an Abraham Lincoln; fear develops an Al Capone.

Faith makes men honorable at trade; fear makes men dishonest and stealthy-minded.

Faith causes one to look for and to find the best there is in men; fear discovers only their shortcomings and deficiencies.

Faith unmistakably identifies itself through the look in one's eyes, the expression on one's face, the tone of one's voice, and the way one walks; fear identifies itself through the same avenues.

Faith attracts only that which is helpful and constructive; fear attracts only that which is destructive.

Right works through faith; wrong works through fear.

Anything that causes one to be afraid should have close examination.

Both faith and fear have a tendency to clothe themselves in physical realities, through the most practical and natural media available.

Faith constructs; fear tears down. The order never is reversed!

> Faith evolves a great leader; fear creates a cringing follower.

Faith and fear never fraternize. Both cannot occupy the mind at the same time. One or the other must, and always does, dominate.

Faith can lift an individual to great heights of achievement in any calling; fear can and does make achievement impossible in any calling.

Fear ushered in the worst panic the world has ever known; faith will usher it out again.

Faith is nature's alchemy with which she mixes and blends the spiritual with the physical and mental forces.

Fear will no more mix with spiritual force than will oil with water.

Faith is every man's privilege. When exercised, it removes most of the real and all of the imagined limitations with which man binds himself in his own mind.

CALL TO
COURAGE

Strengthen your faith by...

- ...always looking for the good in yourself, other people, and the world around you.

- ...remaining steadfast in your pursuit of your definite major purpose.

- ...reinforcing your definite major purpose with definite plans backed by definite action.

- ...constructing a support system that empowers you to persevere through adversity.

- ...identifying and obtaining resources that equip you to weather turbulent times.

- ...finding ways to serve others with your time, talent, and resources.

- ...observing and appreciating the time-tested stability of natural law.

- ...coating your thoughts in the positive emotions of faith, hope, love, and charity until your thought habits become a state of mind.

- ...establishing your values and never deviating from them.

- ...acting with honesty and integrity in all circumstances.

- ...leading and mentoring others to success.

- ...creating a legacy characterized by generosity and service.

1. What specific action steps do you need to take to build faith?

_____

_____

_____

_____

_____

_____

_____

_____

_____

_____

_____

_____

_____

SUSCEPTIBILITY
TO NEGATIVE INFLUENCES

1. Have you identified your definite major purpose? If not, answer the
    following questions:

    - What above all else do you desire?

    _____

    _____

    _____

    _____

    _____

    _____

- What are you willing to give in exchange for attaining it (e.g., time, resources, missed opportunities)?

_____

_____

_____

_____

_____

- By when do you commit to attaining it?

_____

_____

_____

_____

_____

2. Do you have a plan for achieving your definite major purpose? If not, answer the following questions:

- What previous plans could be combined or modified to create a new opportunity?

_____

_____

_____

_____

_____

_____

- What have other successful individuals done to obtain the same result?

_____

_____

_____

_____

_____

_____

- What have you learned from previous failures?

- What counsel has your mastermind offered?

3. Do you avoid the association of any specific person or group, and
    if so, why? List some ways you can learn from them.

    _____

    _____

    _____

    _____

    _____

    _____

4. Do you regularly feel self-conscious? If so, can you identify
    reasons why?

    _____

    _____

    _____

    _____

    _____

    _____

5. Do you like your occupation? If not, can you think of three things you would rather be doing for your career?

_____

_____

_____

_____

_____

_____

6. Have you been able to learn from your previous mistakes? If so, what have some of the lessons been?

_____

_____

_____

_____

_____

_____

7. Are you envious of anyone? If so, why?

_____

_____

_____

_____

_____

_____

8. To what do you devote most of your time? How is this a constructive or destructive use of your time?

_____

_____

_____

_____

_____

_____

9. Can you identify times in your life when you were dwelling on failure? What got you past it? Take note of this and use it as a strategy to overcome the fear of failure.

    _____

    _____

    _____

    _____

    _____

    _____

10. Do you generally feel good or bad physically? Can you identify the cause and make a plan to do more of what makes you feel good?

    _____

    _____

    _____

    _____

    _____

    _____

11. Who has had the most inspiring influence on you, and why?

_____

_____

_____

_____

_____

_____

12. How can you spend more time with them?

_____

_____

_____

_____

_____

_____

13. Do you tolerate negative influences? If so, why?

_____

_____

_____

_____

_____

_____

14. List ways to avoid them.

_____

_____

_____

_____

_____

_____

15. Can you identify situations in which you were easily influenced by others? What was the result?

_____

_____

_____

_____

_____

_____

16. How can you avoid this in the future?

_____

_____

_____

_____

_____

_____

17. Do you schedule time to practice autosuggestion or meditation to make your thoughts more positive? If not, how can you carve out time—starting today—to form better thought habits?

_____

_____

_____

_____

_____

_____

18. What have you learned today, this week, and/or this month that you can use to improve your mindset tomorrow? List at least three things.

_____

_____

_____

_____

_____

_____

19. Can you name three of your biggest weaknesses? What are some possible ways to begin correcting them?

_____

_____

_____

_____

_____

_____

20. Do you change your mind often? If so, why?

_____

_____

_____

_____

_____

21. How can you be bolder and firmer in your decision-making?

22. Do you usually finish everything you begin? If not, why?

23. How can you eliminate the distractions and obstacles that stand in your way?

_____

_____

_____

_____

_____

24. Can you identify your three greatest fears or worries? What would eliminate them?

_____

_____

_____

_____

_____

25. How much time have you devoted to studying and answering these
    questions?

    _____

    _____

    _____

> You have ABSOLUTE
> CONTROL over one thing,
> and that is your thoughts.

If you have answered all these questions truthfully, you know more
about yourself than the majority of people. Study the questions carefully,
come back to them once each week for several months, and be astounded
at the amount of additional knowledge you will have gained by the simple
method of answering the questions truthfully. If you are not certain con-
cerning the answers to some of the questions, seek the counsel of those
who know you well, especially those who have no motive in flattering you,
and see yourself through their eyes. The experience will be astonishing.

This is the most significant and inspiring of all facts known to man!
It reflects man's Divine nature. This Divine prerogative is the sole means
by which you may control your own destiny. If you fail to control your
own mind, you may be sure you will control nothing else.

NOTES

CHAPTER 1

1. Napoleon Hill, *The Master-Key to Riches* (1945; repr., Shippensburg, PA: Sound Wisdom, 2018), 176–77.

2. Ibid., 173.

3. Ibid.

4. Ibid., 174.

5. William Ernest Henley, "Invictus," *Poetry Foundation*, Poetry Foundation, 2020, http://www.poetryfoundation.org/poems/51642/invictus.

6. Napoleon Hill, *Think and Grow Rich* (1937; repr., Shippensburg, PA: Sound Wisdom, 2016), 50.

7. Ibid., 23.

8. Ibid., 44–45.

9. Ibid., 65.

10. Napoleon Hill, "Maker of Miracle Men," in *Napoleon Hill's Greatest Speeches* (Shippensburg, PA: Sound Wisdom, 2016), 208.

11. Hill, *Master-Key*, 17.

12. Hill, *Think and Grow Rich*, 49.

13. Ibid., 45.

CHAPTER 2

1. Hill, *Think and Grow Rich,* 28.

2. Ibid., 20.

3. Napoleon Hill, "The Five Essentials of Success," in *Napoleon Hill's Greatest Speeches* (Shippensburg, PA: Sound Wisdom, 2016), 153.

4. James Hayton and Gabriella Cacciotti, "How Fear Helps (and Hurts) Entrepreneurs," *Harvard Business Review,* April 3, 2018, http://hbr.org/2018/04/how-fear-helps-and-hurts-entrepreneurs.

5. Hill, *Think and Grow Rich,* 47.

6. Ibid., 311.

7. Hill, *Master-Key,* 170.

8. Ibid., 173.

9. Hill, *Think and Grow Rich,* 50.

10. Napoleon Hill, "This Changing World," in *Napoleon Hill's Greatest Speeches* (Shippensburg, PA: Sound Wisdom, 2016), 256.

11. Ibid., 250.

12. Ibid., 256.

13. Hill, *Think and Grow Rich,* 71.

CHAPTER 3

1. Elbert Hubbard qtd. in Dale Carnegie, "How 'Teddy' Roosevelt Conquered Fear," *The Detroit Free Press,* March 17, 1941, 3.

2. Hill, *Think and Grow Rich,* 80–81.

3. Ibid., 81.

4. Franklin D. Roosevelt, "First Inaugural Address," *Archives.gov*, last updated September 23, 2016, http://www.archives.gov/education/lessons/fdr-inaugural.

5. Hill, *Master-Key*, 23.

6. Ibid., 168.

7. Hill, *Think and Grow Rich*, 362.

8. Ibid., 330.

9. The fear of loss of liberty was not one of the original six ghosts of fear identified in *Think and Grow Rich*. Hill added it later, and it appears in his catalog of fears in *The Master-Key to Riches*, 23.

10. Hill, *Think and Grow Rich*, 332.

11. Ibid., 330.

12. Ibid.

13. Amy McKeever, "Coronavirus Is Spreading Panic. Here's the Science Behind Why," *National Geographic*, March 17, 2020, http://www.nationalgeographic.com/history/reference/modern-history/why-we-evolved-to-feel-panic-anxiety/.

14. Hill, *Think and Grow Rich*, 345–46.

15. McKeever, "Coronavirus."

16. Hill, *Think and Grow Rich,* 345.

CHAPTER 4

1. Ralph Waldo Emerson, "Courage," in *Society and Solitude: Twelve Chapters* (Boston: Fields, Osgood, & Co., 1870), 247.

2. Hill, *Think and Grow Rich*, 356.

3. Ibid., 234.

4. This book on fear is not intended to diagnose or treat phobias, panic disorders, or other medical conditions. Please consult a trained medical professional for medical advice.

5.   Hill, *Master-Key*, 236.
6.   Hill, *Think and Grow Rich*, 257.
7.   Hill, *Master-Key*, 237.
8.   Ibid.

CHAPTER 5

1.   Hill, *Master-Key*, 111.
2.   Hill, *Think and Grow Rich*, 256.
3.   Hill, *Master-Key*, 112.
4.   Napoleon Hill, "The Five Essentials of Success," in *Napoleon Hill's Greatest Speeches* (Shippensburg, PA: Sound Wisdom, 2016), 174.
5.   Hill, *Think and Grow Rich*, 297.
6.   Ibid., 46.

CHAPTER 6

1.   This is an excerpt from "This Changing World," an article Napoleon Hill wrote during the Great Depression, likely near the end of 1930, and published in *Plain Talk* magazine. It was reprinted in *Napoleon Hill's Greatest Speeches* (Shippensburg, PA: Sound Wisdom, 2016), 249–58. This excerpt appears on pp. 256–57.

ABOUT THE AUTHOR

NAPOLEON HILL was born in 1883 in a one-room cabin on the Pound River in Wise County, Virginia. He began his writing career at age 13 as a "mountain reporter" for small town newspapers and went on to become America's most beloved motivational author. Hill passed away in November 1970 after a long and successful career writing, teaching, and lecturing about the principles of success. Dr. Hill's work stands as a monument to individual achievement and is the cornerstone of modern motivation. His book, Think and Grow Rich, is the all-time bestseller in the field. Hill established the Foundation as a nonprofit educational institution whose mission is to perpetuate his philosophy of leadership, self-motivation, and individual achievement. His books, audio cassettes, videotapes, and other motivational products are made available to you as a service of the Foundation so that you may build your own library of personal achievement materials...and help you acquire financial wealth and the true riches of life.

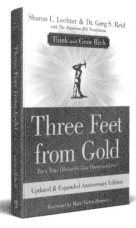

ADDITIONAL TITLES FROM THE NAPOLEON HILL FOUNDATION

Freedom from Your Fears

Gift of Giving

Law of Success

Magic Ladder to Success

Master-Key to Riches

Napoleon Hill's Action Activities for Health, Wealth and Happiness

Napoleon Hill's Gold Standard

Napoleon Hill's Greatest Speeches

Napoleon Hill's Keys to Personal Achievement

Napoleon Hill's Life Lessons

Napoleon Hill's Positive Thinking

Napoleon Hill's Power of Positive Action

Napoleon Hill's Self-Confidence Formula

Napoleon Hill's Success Principles Rediscovered

Outwitting the Devil

Success and Something Greater

Think and Grow Rich

Think and Grow Rich: The Legacy

Three Feet from Gold

The Law of Success

soundwisdom.com/naphill

Printed in Great Britain
by Amazon

60364399R00078